11/14

INSIDE OUTER SPACE

SOLAR Systems

Nadia Higgins

Rourke
Educational Media

rourkeeducationalmedia.com

Scan for Related Titles and Teacher Resources

Teaching Focus:

Fluency: Using Expression- Have students read aloud to practice reading with expression and with appropriate pacing.

Before Reading:

Building Academic Vocabulary and Background Knowledge

Before reading a book, it is important to set the stage for your child or student by using pre-reading strategies. This will help them develop their vocabulary, increase their reading comprehension, and make connections across the curriculum.

1. Read the title and look at the cover. *Let's make predictions about what this book will be about.*
2. Take a picture walk by talking about the pictures/photographs in the book. Implant the vocabulary as you take the picture walk. Be sure to talk about the text features such as headings, Table of Contents, glossary, bolded words, captions, charts/diagrams, or Index.
3. Have students read the first page of text with you then have students read the remaining text.
4. Strategy Talk – use to assist students while reading.
   - Get your mouth ready
   - Look at the picture
   - Think…does it make sense
   - Think…does it look right
   - Think…does it sound right
   - Chunk it – by looking for a part you know
5. Read it again.
6. After reading the book complete the activities below.

Content Area Vocabulary
Use glossary words in a sentence.

astronomers
exoplanets
gravity
light years
orbit
solar system

After Reading:

Comprehension and Extension Activity

After reading the book, work on the following questions with your child or students in order to check their level of reading comprehension and content mastery.

1. Why are scientists searching for exoplanets like ours? *(Asking questions)*
2. What are the two types of planets in our solar system? *(Summarize)*
3. When we are walking down the street, why don't we float away? *(Text to self connection)*
4. Where do planets get their light from? *(Summarize)*

Extension Activity

Using various art supplies make a diagram of our solar system. You can use markers, paper, balls, candy, glitter, or anything else that helps you visually show the solar system to your classmates. This diagram should show the planets in relationship to each other and to the Sun. Be sure to title your diagram and label each of the eight planets.

Table of Contents

A New View of the Universe

In 1992, two **astronomers** answered a question people had been asking for hundreds of years. Do other stars besides our Sun have planets?

Yes, the scientists said. They had found three planets around a distant star—another **solar system**!

In 1994, astronomers confirmed that three planets orbit the distant star PSRB1257+12.

Since then, scientists have found hundreds of stars with planets. They believe billions of solar systems fill outer space.

So Far Away!
Our closest solar system is about 10 **light years** away. That means a beam of light would take 10 years to get there. The trip would take 100 million years in a car!

7

Sun

How Solar Systems Work

Scientists use our own solar system as a model for others.

The Sun shines in the center. It is so huge, the planets seem tiny next to it.

Our solar system has two main types of planets. Some are small and rocky, like Earth.

Earth

Other planets are giant balls of gas, like Jupiter. All planets get their light from the Sun.

Jupiter

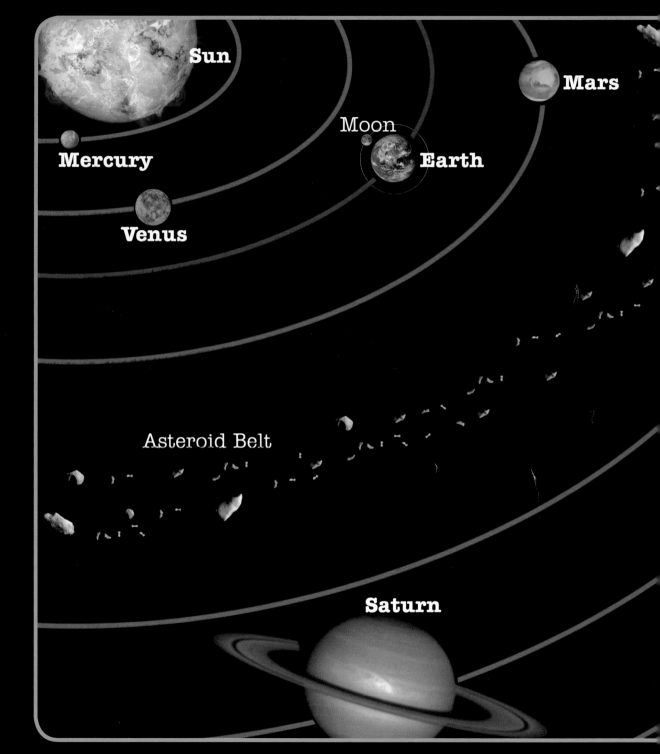

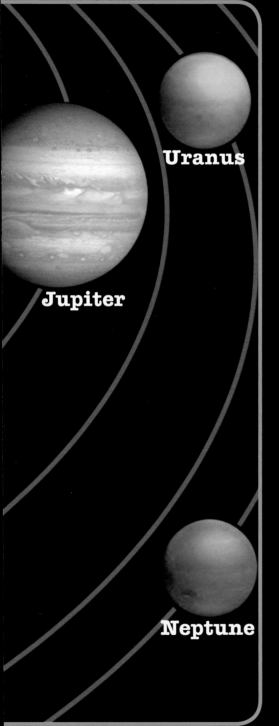

Uranus

Jupiter

Neptune

The planets **orbit** the Sun. Each planet travels on its own oval path.

For billions of years, the planets have kept to their orderly places.

Why don't the planets spin away? **Gravity** keeps them in their places.

On Earth, this important force pulls things to the ground. That's why we don't float away! In space, the Sun and planets also pull on each other.

How Solar Systems Form
A solar system begins as a spinning cloud of gas and dust. Gravity pulls the cloud into a ball, making a star. Planets form from what's left over.

Sun

The pull of gravity keeps the planets, moons, and other objects in our solar system from spinning away.

Amazing Discoveries

Exoplanets of faraway suns have scientists scratching their heads. Some of these distant planets would never work in our own solar system. They are too big. Or they orbit too fast. Some are just plain weird!

Scientists were excited to find three small planets around star KOI-961. That showed how powerful their telescopes could be.

WEIRD PLANETS!

Planet	Oddball Characteristics
55 Cancri e	A thick layer of diamond lies under the surface.
HD 188753 Ab	Three suns set in the sky.
TrES-2b	Barely any light shines in this pitch black world.
HAT-P-1b	This giant is as light as Styrofoam.
HD 189733b	It rains glass.
Kepler-78b	One year takes $8\frac{1}{2}$ hours.

In 2005, scientists found a planet that orbits a solar system with three stars. It is very close to the central star, completing an orbit in less than 4 days!

19

Searching the skies, scientists have even found a planet very much like Earth. The planet, Kepler-186f, is small and rocky. It is not too hot or too cold. It is even possible that this alien world could host life, like our own amazing planet.

What else will scientists discover in outer space?

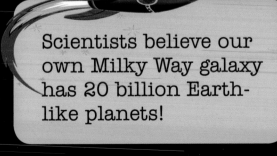

Scientists believe our own Milky Way galaxy has 20 billion Earth-like planets!

Scientists will have to study Kepler-186f to find out how likely it is to have life.

Could There Be Life?

To find out if a planet is the right temperature for life, scientists ask five main questions.

How hot is the star?

How far away is the planet from its star?

How old is the planet?

What's the air like?

Does the planet have water?

Photo Glossary

astronomers (uh-STRON-uh-muhrz): Scientists who study outer space are astronomers.

exoplanets (ehk-soh-PLAN-ihtz): Planets in solar systems other than our own are exoplanets.

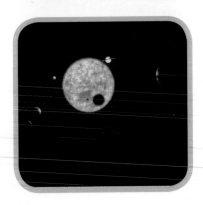

gravity (GRAV-uh-tee): Gravity is a force in the universe that pulls objects toward each other.

light years (LYT YIHRZ): Scientists measure the distance between stars in light years. One light year is the distance it takes light to travel in one year.

orbit (AWR-biht): When something has an orbit, it travels in a round path around something else.

solar system (SOH-luhr SIHS-tuhm): The solar system is made of a star and all the planets and other space objects that travel around it.

Index

Websites

planetquest.jpl.nasa.gov/interactives
spaceplace.nasa.gov/menu/solar-system/
www.planetary.org/multimedia/video/
    consider/how-can-we-find.html

Meet The Author!
www.meetREMauthors.com

About the Author

Nadia Higgins is the author of more than 70 books for kids. She has written about everything from ants to zombies, but space topics are her very favorite. Higgins lives in Minneapolis, Minnesota, with her husband and two daughters.

PHOTO CREDITS: Cover © ESO/M. Kornmesser, http://www.eso.org/public/images/eso1204a/; page 5 courtesy NASA; page 7 © ESO/M. Kornmesser, http://www.eso.org/public/images/eso1204a/; page 8-9 © Bobboz; page 10 and 11 © Tristan3D; page 12-13 © ktynzq; page 15 © Sebastian Kaulitzki; page 16-17 © Image credit: NASA/JPL-Caltech; page 19 courtesy JPL-Caltech, NASA; page 20 courtesy of NASA Ames/SETI Institute/JPL-Caltech; page 22 top and middle photos NASA/JPL-Caltech, bottom © Sebastian Kaulitzki; page 23 top © ESO/M. Kornmesser, http://www.eso.org/public/images/eso1204a/, middle © ktynzq, bottom © Bobboz

Edited by: Jill Sherman

Cover design and Interior design: by Nicola Stratford
nicolastratford.com

Library of Congress PCN Data

Solar Systems / Nadia Higgins
(Inside Outer Space)
ISBN 978-1-62717-730-6 (hard cover)
ISBN 978-1-62717-852-5 (soft cover)
ISBN 978-1-62717-964-5 (e-Book)
Library of Congress Control Number: 2014935656

Rourke Educational Media
Printed in the United States of America, North Mankato, Minnesota

Also Available as:

ROURKE'S
e-Books